There was an old woman
who swallowed a **spider**,
That wriggled and jiggled
and tickled inside her,
She swallowed the spider
to catch the fly,
I don't know why
she swallowed the fly,
Perhaps she'll die.

There was an old woman
who swallowed a **bird,**
How absurd!
to swallow a bird,
She swallowed the bird
to catch the spider,
That wriggled and jiggled
and tickled inside her,
She swallowed the spider
to catch the fly,
I don't know why
she swallowed the fly,
Perhaps she'll die.

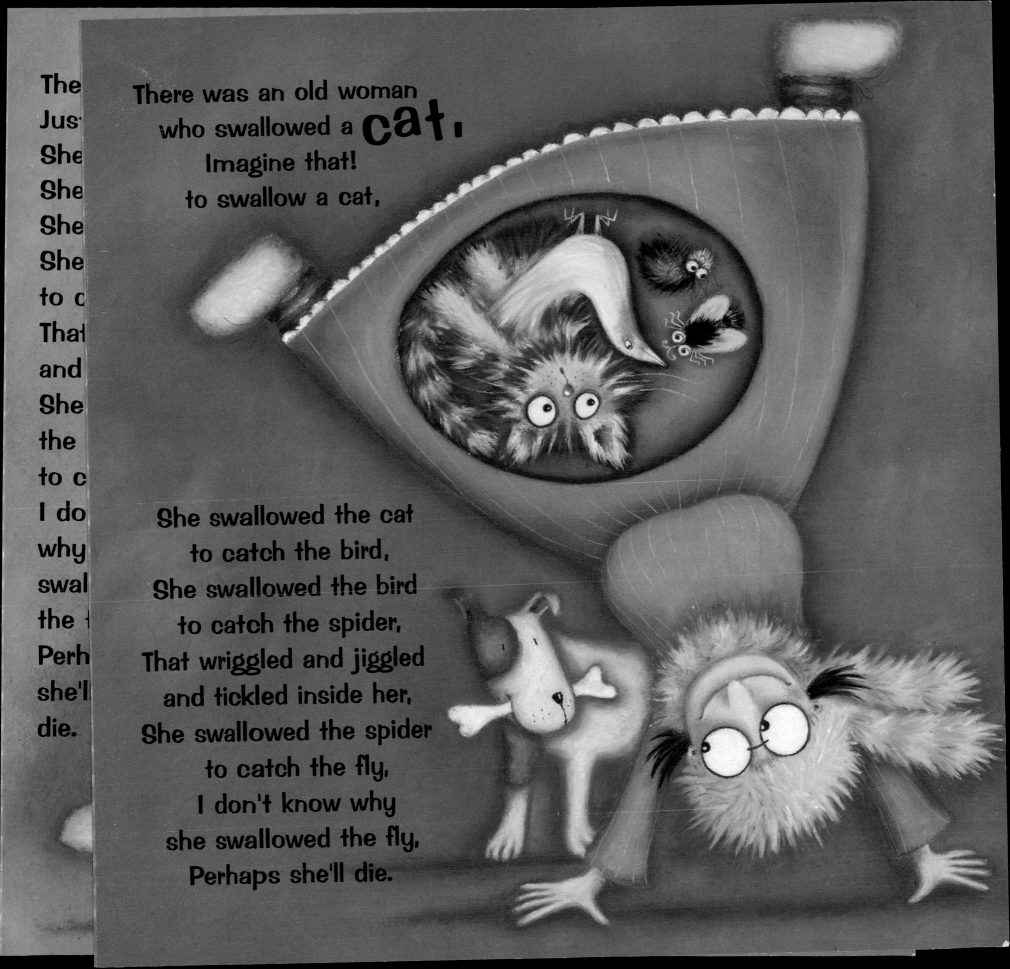

There was an old woman
who swallowed a **cat,**
Imagine that!
to swallow a cat,

She swallowed the cat
to catch the bird,
She swallowed the bird
to catch the spider,
That wriggled and jiggled
and tickled inside her,
She swallowed the spider
to catch the fly,
I don't know why
she swallowed the fly,
Perhaps she'll die.

There was an
old woman who
swallowed a COW,
I don't know how
she swallowed a cow!
She swallowed the cow
to catch the goat,
She swallowed the goat
to catch the dog,
She swallowed the dog
to catch the cat,
She swallowed the cat to catch the bird,
She swallowed the bird to catch the spider,
That wriggled and jiggled and tickled inside her,
She swallowed the spider to catch the fly,
I don't know why she swallowed the fly,
Perhaps she'll die.

There was
an old woman
who swallowed a
horse.